Meditation Journal
For Anxiety

Daily Meditations,
Prompts, and Practices
for Finding Calm

Peter J. Economou, PhD, ABPP

**ROCKRIDGE
PRESS**

For general information on our other products and services or to obtain technical support, please contact our Customer Care Department within the United States at (866) 744-2665, or outside the United States at (510) 253-0500.

Rockridge Press publishes its books in a variety of electronic and print formats. Some content that appears in print may not be available in electronic books, and vice versa.

TRADEMARKS: Rockridge Press and the Rockridge Press logo are trademarks or reg-istered trademarks of Callisto Media Inc. and/or its affiliates, in the United States and other countries, and may not be used without written permission. All other trademarks are the property of their respective owners. Rockridge Press is not associated with any product or vendor mentioned in this book.

Interior and Cover Designer: Scott Petrower
Art Producer: Hannah Dickerson
Editor: John Makowski
Production Editor: Emily Sheehan
Production Manager: Jose Olivera

All illustrations used under license from Shutterstock.com and iStock.com
Author photo courtesy of Leigh Castelli Photography

ISBN: Print 978-1-64876-975-7
R0

This journal belongs to:

....

Introduction

Life is full of surprises—like riding a roller coaster. There are ups and downs and sharp turns, and at times we feel like we are upside down. Anyone who has had intense feelings of anxiety can relate, and such feelings have likely brought you to this meditation journal. Meditation can improve your life, but you will still feel anxiety at times. That is because anxiety is a basic emotion that we all experience. If anxiety has been controlling your life, this book can help you gain new perspectives and build strength to help you live a balanced and peaceful life. That is what meditation has done for me and my own anxiety.

As a competitive swimmer, I would become sick before races and elite competitions. It was just routine. I would warm up, stretch, go to the bathroom and get sick, get behind the blocks, and race. This was not healthy, nor was it effective. After I started to meditate during my undergraduate years, I would get sick less often before competitions. By senior year, I never once became sick, even as I competed at the Olympic trials. I had built a healthy relationship with my anxiety. Today, I am a psychologist practicing in the New York City area, a professor of psychology, and a dharma holder within Zen Buddhism.

My practice of meditation within Zen Buddhism teachings, under the direction of Robert Kennedy Roshi, has yielded tremendous benefits in my life. It has improved my personal, familial, and professional relationships; decreased my stress and anxiety; enhanced my general well-being; and so much more. I have been able to incorporate meditation into my clinical work through evidenced-based cognitive behavioral therapies, thereby helping others transform their lives. This has included clinical work in private practice, integration into sport psychology with professional and collegiate athletes as well as corporate high performers, and enhancing the classroom experience for graduate students training in psychology. I have also been involved in research utilizing meditation as an intervention, which has produced valuable findings.

A lot of research has demonstrated that meditation has many benefits, especially easing anxiety. As early as the 1970s, John Kabat-Zinn began studying mindfulness for chronic pain. Through this work, the protocol *mindfulness-based stress reduction* (MBSR) was born and has since been studied time and again. Fast-forward to the 21st century, where we have found that meditation can reduce stress hormones, decrease inflammation that causes disease, and improve the ability to cope with anxiety and stress.

This journal will help you foster your own meditation practice and build a healthier relationship with your feelings of anxiety. It will provide you with one practice for each day of the week. Try to do only one practice each day. The process of building a meditation practice is not done quickly (nor is it easy), so it is important to pace yourself. This book follows the general outline I use when working with clients, focusing on the mind, body, and spirit. The weeks are clustered into parts; you will practice meditation related to the mind first, then the body, and finally the spirit. I have created a theme for each week (or each color-coded set of seven prompts), so you will notice that the prompts within each week are related.

Whether this is your first time doing meditation or you have tried meditation previously, this book will contribute to your practice. I encourage you to be patient, stay curious, and focus on making a commitment to your personal growth and well-being.

Meditations to Return To

In life, we sometimes get lost. When we do, some of us ask for directions, some figure it out on their own, and others panic. If you feel lost or stuck at any time, return to this space. The three meditations that follow are meant to help redirect you, because it is possible that as you build your meditation practice, you may get lost. Consider coming back here when you notice that you have lost your way.

Releasing Control

Though we may think we are in control, sometimes something bigger than us wins. Think about a trip you had planned before the 2020 pandemic that got cancelled. There was that race you prepared for like never before, and days before the race, you got injured and could not participate. You prepared yourself for a difficult conversation with a loved one or your boss, but then during the conversation, you could not contain your emotions and cried.

Once we can release the need to be in control, we can find peace. Practice saying "I release control." Find a practice that feels best for you, whether it is repeating these words internally as a mantra, aloud in front of a mirror, outside while in nature, or some other practice. Repeating this phrase is meant to be liberating and uncomfortable.

Belly Breathing

At any given time, in any situation, you can always count your breaths. For this meditation, focus on taking six deep belly breaths, inhaling and exhaling in equal amounts. As you inhale, push your belly out like there is a balloon in your belly. As you exhale, bring your belly button back toward your spine. Repeat this for six breaths, focusing on the rise and fall of your belly. Every time your mind wanders, bring it back to focus on the rise and fall of your belly. You can do this practice while walking, sitting, or standing.

Color Visualization

In a comfortable seated position, begin with a few deep breaths and allow your eyes to close. Assume a gentle rhythm with your breathing. As you inhale, try to visualize one of the colors in a rainbow. You may begin to visualize different shades of the color or objects that match it. Observe what you are feeling in response to the color. As you exhale, let go of any negative emotions that may arise that do not serve you in a positive way. Repeat with each color of the rainbow, then bring your attention back to your breath.

PART ONE

MIND

Meditation teaches us that we are not what we think. As we build our meditation practice, one goal is to build a heathy relationship with our mind. Our inner dialogue is constant and can be distracting. Beginning in the 1970s, researchers learned that meditation could decrease anxiety, and a review of the literature by Delmonte in 1985 confirmed that people who meditated regularly reported less anxiety. Our relationship with our thoughts impacts how we meditate, as well as our overall well-being. Let us begin understanding our mind.

Find a comfortable seated position. Set your shoulders above your hips and your knees above your ankles. Bring your attention to your feet on the ground. Set a timer for three minutes and focus on your feet. See if you can notice the sock around your foot, your foot in your shoe, your shoe on the ground. Sometimes I think of an itch, which often creates a small tickle. Can you imagine a slight tickle on your ankle?

Below, write down all of the observations that come to mind about your body.

Look at the words you wrote yesterday about your body. Choose one of the words. Use it as a mantra. Repeat this word over and over, either aloud or internally. If your word is negative, that is okay. The more you repeat this word, the less powerful it becomes. Words and thoughts are just that. They do not necessarily reflect reality.

What did you notice during this practice?

....

....

....

....

....

....

....

....

....

....

....

....

....

We all judge. The practice of meditation brings awareness of our judgments. However, this can create a vicious cycle: we become aware of the judgment, we experience guilt for having that thought, we overcompensate for our thoughts, and then we go back to the judgment.

Today, notice your judgment cycles. The aim is to break them over time. Start by describing one of your cycles here.

....

....

....

....

....

....

....

....

....

....

....

....

....

"I AM NOT WHAT I THINK."

Reflect on your thoughts after you meditate today.

Yesterday's meditation included a statement without any accompanying instructions. Write down your reactions and thoughts and how you interpreted that statement.

Can you increase your meditation time today? For the first prompt this week I suggested sitting for three to five minutes. For today, set your timer for 5 to 10 minutes. Notice all of the thoughts that come and go. Simply sit, notice, and release. It is like fishing just for fun—catch and release.

What did you notice as you tried to "catch and release"?

This week we learned that we are not what we think. Learning this takes time and practice. Each week, consider your intentions and create a goal about your practice of meditation. Try to gradually increase the time spent meditating as you progress through the weeks in this journal.

What are your goals for the next week?

....

....

....

....

....

....

....

....

....

....

....

....

....

Worry thoughts are common and are a part of the internal dialogue we have when we feel nervous, anxious, or fearful. The goal of today's practice is to raise awareness of our worry thoughts and how they affect our body. This will help reduce the amount of time spent worrying.

Write down some worry thoughts that you have.

....

....

....

....

....

Now, describe where in your body you feel worry.

....

....

....

....

....

Sit in an upright position, shoulders above your hips and knees above your ankles, with your spine straight and the crown of your head lifted toward the sky.

Review the thoughts that you wrote down yesterday. Let them come in, then go out. Practice noticing them and letting them pass from your mind. Do this for at least five minutes.

What did you notice during this practice?

....

....

....

....

....

....

....

....

....

....

....

....

It is normal to worry but, like many things, too much of it is unhealthy. Today you are allowed to have five minutes to worry. You have to say your worry thoughts aloud, though. Look in a mirror, set a timer for five minutes, and speak your worry thoughts without judging them.

Describe what it felt like to speak your worry thoughts out loud.

....

....

....

....

....

....

....

....

....

....

....

....

....

Set your timer for whatever limit feels good for you today. Sit in a comfortable position and simply repeat "I release worry" for the allotted time as you breathe naturally. Think of this as being like a prayer or mantra. Ignore any distracting thoughts by continuing to repeat the mantra. When the timer goes off, end the meditation with a few deep breaths.

Reflect on this experience below.

The goal of meditation is to recognize how powerful our thoughts are. Through meditation, we learn that worrying is simply a behavior we can improve on.

What have you learned about your worry thoughts to this point?

Worry thoughts are like a hamster running on a wheel. They are physically taxing, but the energy expended doesn't get us anywhere. As you meditate today, try to slow down the hamster wheel by allowing your worry thoughts to come and go without trying to change them.

Reflect on this practice below.

Remember to reflect on the role of worry in your life and continue to incorporate these practices. The worry in front of a mirror exercise, for instance, is very helpful for decreasing worry over time. It just takes practice.

How did this week's exercises resonate with you?
Which ones are you most likely to do again?

Have you noticed the impact music has on your body? People often use music to distract themselves from the internal noise of their thoughts. Meditation can help lower the volume of thoughts.

Choose your favorite music playlist, then just sit, listen, and observe. Select different songs and see how your body responds to them. Record your observations below.

....

....

....

....

....

....

....

....

....

....

....

....

....

On a mobile device or computer, search for the following keywords: "liquid mind" or "meditation music" or "concentration for studying." When you find a piece of music, just sit and listen to it; do nothing else. Preferably, the music you choose will not have words. The purpose of this exercise is to separate yourself from your thoughts.

Try this for up to 10 minutes. How did it feel to separate from your thoughts?

....

....

....

....

....

....

....

....

....

....

....

....

....

How did you feel the past two days while attempting to perform an exercise without any distractions? Initially, it can feel odd, but with practice we start to yearn for that quiet time.

Without judgment, write down what you noticed (in your mind or body, or both) while performing these exercises.

....

....

....

....

....

....

....

....

....

....

....

....

....

"I CAN CONTROL THE VOLUME."

Use this phrase as a mantra as you meditate.
How loud were your thoughts?

Review the phrase you repeated during yesterday's meditation. What are your thoughts about this phrase? What does it mean to you?

Did you find a playlist you liked earlier this week? If so, listen to it today for at least 10 minutes. Remember: find music, without words, that impacts your body and just sit and listen. No phones, no texting or emailing, and no talking. Your goal is to keep building this practice.

Write down the playlists or songs you have used thus far. Were there any that you found particularly impactful?

....

....

....

....

....

....

....

....

....

....

....

....

....

Meditation can help lower the volume of our thoughts, which allows anxious feelings and moments to become less painful in time. Keep noticing the volume level of your thoughts during times of suffering and practice meditating to lower the volume.

WHAT IS THE VOLUME OF YOUR THOUGHTS DURING MOMENTS OF ANXIETY?

(1) (2) (3) (4) (5) (6) (7) (8) (9) (10)

HOW LOUD IS THE VOLUME WHEN YOU START MEDITATING?

(1) (2) (3) (4) (5) (6) (7) (8) (9) (10)

WHAT DO YOUR THOUGHTS "SOUND LIKE" DURING MOMENTS OF ANXIETY VERSUS WHEN YOU'RE MEDITATING?

....

....

....

....

....

....

....

....

....

Many people believe the mind is in the brain. But we are not sure where it is, which is why there is research on consciousness. The thoughts in our mind could be in our toes, heart, or stomach, or even outside our body. As we become more aware of our thoughts, we become more attuned to the connection between the mind and the body.

Today, sit and notice where your mind is. Where do you think it is located? How can you tell?

Set a timer for 10 minutes. Sitting upright with your feet resting on the floor, close your eyes and focus on the natural rhythm of your breathing. Observe when your mind wanders, and when it does, simply return your attention back to your breathing.

Reflect on how your mind is feeling.

Because we all make judgments, it is time to accept our judging mind. Acceptance of our judgments brings about inner peace, and today we will practice neutral judgment.

In the following table, write down some judgments, and then practice transforming each judgment into a neutral one.

JUDGMENT	NEUTRAL JUDGMENT
That spaghetti was terrible and overcooked.	I ate spaghetti that my spouse made.

Sit (or lie down) and ponder your mind. Earlier this week, we looked at where it might be located. Now, just be with your mind. Watch it. Turn your attention inward. Imagine a space behind your mind's eye and allow any negative thoughts to soften and dissolve. Try doing this for 10 minutes.

What thoughts kept coming up for you?

....

....

....

....

....

....

....

....

....

....

....

....

....

Many of us do not want to let go of our judging mind, and some people even think they will enjoy life less without it. Earlier this week, as you transformed judgments to be more neutral, did you notice that the effort feels flat at first, as if you are taking the joy out of experiences? That is common, but over time it becomes more fulfilling.

*Write down your feelings about
letting go of judging.*

....

....

....

....

....

....

....

....

....

....

....

....

....

Color the picture below, slowly, mindfully, and without judgment. Avoid paying too much attention to the colors you choose and trying to make it perfect.

How was this experience for you? What do you judge about your coloring?

....

....

....

....

....

....

This week, we were philosophical about the mind and consciousness. We learned about judgments, and we colored! All of these can be seen as meditative practices. Meditation does not mean sitting cross-legged with eyes closed, alone in the mountains. Meditation is whatever you want it to be, and learning to release control of the mind makes meditation practices richer.

What are some examples of meditation you have used to this point?

Though we may think we are in control, sometimes something bigger than us wins. Once we can relinquish the need and desire to be in control—especially of our thoughts—we can find peace.

Recall a time when you felt prepared, then lost control. How did your mind and body respond?

....

....

....

....

....

....

....

....

....

....

....

....

....

"I RELEASE CONTROL."

Repeat this phrase internally as a mantra. If you choose, you could also repeat this phrase aloud in front of a mirror, while walking outside or hiking in nature, while lying down, or anywhere you are comfortable. Find a practice that feels best for you. This phrase is meant to be liberating and uncomfortable.

How do you imagine your life would be if you were able to release control?

....

....

....

....

....

....

....

....

....

....

....

....

We all have thoughts like "If I completely prepare, then nothing can go wrong." We have also experienced times when being prepared or in control has helped us. This makes letting go of control difficult. But the benefits of letting go outweigh the costs.

How do you feel about giving up control?
What are the pros and cons of letting go?

PROS	CONS

Meditation requires patience, curiosity, and commitment. You will come across these words repeatedly in this book. Meditation also requires willingness. Today, observe your willingness to practice, and challenge the time you commit for meditation. Try to increase that time today.

What kind of willpower do you notice in your life generally? How does your willingness impact your behaviors?

....

....

....

....

....

....

....

....

....

....

....

....

....

Ego is a psychological term that refers to how we see ourselves and often includes our level of self-esteem. Part of the ego can be healthy, while other parts can lead to destructive behaviors.

How do you define ego?

....

....

....

....

....

....

Now think of examples of how your ego interfered with some aspect of your life. Don't feel limited by the lines below. Use an extra sheet of paper if necessary.

....

....

....

....

....

If you are someone who likes things to be in their place or "just so," it may annoy you to see a crooked picture on a wall, car keys on the countertop, the toilet seat left up, or dirt on the floor. Today, when you find something out of place, simply leave it there. Stare at it. Be aware of your desire to correct it. The more we can practice letting go of control, the greater peace we will experience.

How did this practice feel for you?

....

....

....

....

....

....

....

....

....

....

....

....

Being able to observe thoughts rather than latching on and trying to control them can change your life. It is the practice of letting go that fosters growth and creates inner peace. Keep tabs on your relationship with the desire to control as you progress through this book.

What are two things you are holding on to from the past? What are two fears you have about the future?

....

....

....

....

....

....

....

....

....

....

....

....

....

Many of us with unhealthy relationships with anxiety are often seen as "overanalyzers" or "overthinkers." We think of all the possible scenarios (or so we imagine) for a situation, but then something else happens that changes the outcome. Then we are surprised and frustrated because things have not worked out the way we planned.

Think of a time when you were (1) overthinking, (2) overanalyzing, (3) ruminating, or (4) obsessing. Explain the situation and describe how your body felt during and after it.

....

....

....

....

....

....

....

....

....

....

....

In the following table, write down the first word that comes to your mind when you read the word(s) in the left column. Then, select one of your words you've written. Repeat it internally or say it aloud (whichever works best for you) as you breathe in and breathe out. Take note of any thoughts and feelings that may surface.

PROMPTING WORD(S)	YOUR WORD
To-do List	
Organization	
Beach	
Planning	
Forest	

*What are your judgments about someone
you believe overthinks or overanalyzes? The
person might be someone in your life, such as a
romantic partner, coworker, or family member.
What do you think of them in terms of how
they process information and approach life?*

Body scans help bring us into the present moment. You can do one sitting, standing, or lying down, with your eyes closed. As you scan upward, starting from your feet, bring your attention to each part of your body—through your legs, torso, arms, and head, and back down again—noticing any sensations you feel without trying to change them. If your mind wanders, simply bring it back to the meditation.

What kind of sensations came up for you?

....

....

....

....

....

....

....

....

....

....

....

....

....

Through meditation, we learn that suffering is caused by holding on to something from the past or worrying about the future. Noticing how we analyze situations brings about a desire to release this obsessive thinking. We want to make lists and to plan, but we do not want those lists and planning to hijack our peace.

*How has past and future analyzing
helped or hindered your peace?*

....

....

....

....

....

....

....

....

....

....

....

....

Commit to meditating for 15 minutes today. You can use a practice from a previous week or your own meditation practice. Just commit to 15 minutes.

How was this time commitment for you?
Was it easy or difficult? How so?

....
....
....
....
....
....
....
....
....
....
....
....
....
....

There is good and bad in all things. Through the practice of meditation, we begin to find the middle path. Recognize that there is more peace when we can find that middle, or gray, area. Whether you find that you analyze or overanalyze, embrace where you are. Have no judgment about who you are.

Describe a time when you were able to find the middle path.

....

....

....

....

....

....

....

....

....

....

....

....

One of the main practices in cognitive behavioral therapy (CBT) is recognizing that thoughts are sometimes irrational, distorted, or dysfunctional. Your thoughts about anxiety are exactly like that. Consider this: no one has ever died from anxiety. Yet, when we feel anxious sensations in our body (e.g., sweating, fast heartbeat, stomachache, etc.), we are convinced that we are about to die.

Today, reflect on how you felt during your last three unhealthy episodes of anxiety.

As you learn how distorted your thoughts can be, take a moment to watch them. Try to simply sit, watch, and observe for at least 10 minutes (or an amount you are more comfortable with).

Allow distorted thoughts to come in, then gently bring your attention back to your breathing.

Which thoughts kept coming back to you?

Write a letter to one of your scarier thoughts. Perhaps it is a thought about dying during a panic attack, or a trip you cancelled because you were too anxious to fly, or a holiday dinner you avoided because too many people would be there. Whatever it is, write a letter to yourself in that moment. Practice compassion and nonjudgment, and encourage that self to release the fear.

"I AM NOT MY THOUGHTS."

How did you react to this phrase?
How does it feel to have no further
instructions for today's meditation?

....

....

....

....

....

....

....

....

....

....

....

....

....

How do you feel at this point in the journal? What have you noticed about your thoughts? Have you practiced less judgment? Are you able to notice your thoughts more, rather than engage with distorted thoughts and judgments?

Today, see if you can bring your attention to gratitude for the mind. Place your focus on the space between your eyes. Referred to as the third eye chakra, this area is known to connect your mind with the external world; with anxiety, we are often too connected. Just breathe and focus on that space for 15 to 20 minutes.

Use the space below to record your thoughts and feelings about this practice.

This is the last day of the cluster of prompts for the mind. Remember, we are working on our mind, body, and spirit. As we move forward, we will connect more deeply with our body.

Reflect back on the past seven weeks, noting your trials, triumphs, and tribulations.

PART TWO
BODY

In this section we will learn to accept
our body. Most of us do not, and that is
because so many of us are uncomfortable in our body. This is due to how we
perceive it looks, messages that others
have given us about our body throughout our lives, or how we feel in it. With
meditation, we learn to just sit in our
body. It is common for this to be painful, both physically and mentally. When
sitting cross-legged for hours, we can
expect that our legs will fall asleep,
but the practice is to observe as they
awake. Over the next seven weeks, we
will investigate our body.

Write down the physical sensations (e.g., sweaty palms, shallow breaths, etc.) you feel when you experience moments of anxiety. Describe the sensations in as much detail as you can.

....

....

....

....

....

....

....

....

....

....

....

....

....

....

....

Sit or lie down and observe one of the physical sensations you wrote about yesterday. For example, if you wrote "sweaty palms," sit upright, palms turned up, and observe your palms. Notice the air on them and see if they began to sweat as you focus on that area. Try to do this practice for 5 to 10 minutes.

What sensation did you observe? What was it like to mindfully observe this sensation?

....

....

....

....

....

....

....

....

....

....

....

....

Many clients come to me after they have tried unsuccessfully to eliminate anxiety through other therapies, medications, substances, food, or other means. The most effective part of meditation for anxiety is accepting it. Anxiety is never going to go away, but you can learn how to manage it.

How do you feel about the fact that you cannot eliminate anxiety?

....

....

....

....

....

What are two ways you can practice to accept it?

....

....

....

....

....

....

Belly breathing is one of the most effective techniques for calming the body. Today, just sit and observe your breathing. You can focus on the rise and fall of your belly; you could also focus on the air moving in and out of your nostrils or simply count your breaths. Each time your mind wanders, gently bring it back to your breathing.

Where did you find your mind wandering to?

Take a moment to think about how you see yourself. Is "anxious" one of the words you would use to describe yourself? If you find this difficult, it can help to first think about how your loved ones or coworkers see you. Reflect on how they would describe you below.

Once we build our practice of meditation, we connect with things on a deeper level—so much so, I find myself saying "Who cares?" a lot. "Who cares how people see me? Who cares that I feel anxiety?" This attitude is a practice of acceptance. Today, sit and love your body just as it is. Use this phrase (or another, if you have one) as a mantra in your meditation today.

How was it to practice gratitude for your body?

....

....

....

....

....

....

....

....

....

....

....

....

....

Begin to notice throughout each day how bodily sensations can hijack your peace. For instance, imagine you're waiting in a line and it is moving slowly. You become hot. Then a thought about escaping enters your mind. These sensations can distract you and keep you from connecting with a stranger in the line. Try to pay attention to your body in the coming weeks.

What is one observation you noticed about your body over the past few weeks?

Over time, an unhealthy relationship with anxiety can lead to chronic pain, headaches, stomach issues, and much more. Using the space below, describe where in your body you feel anxiety most often. Then reflect on the physical sensations you experience.

Meditation has taught us that accepting our body as it is can help us recover from ailments and improve our health. Research has shown that compassion for our body can also improve our recovery from injury. Today, sit for 10 to 15 minutes and feel compassion or gratitude for a part of your body.

Write a thank-you note to that part of your body.

....

....

....

....

....

....

....

....

....

....

....

....

....

....

We all judge our body. Write down some of the first thoughts that come to your mind when you think about your body:

....

....

....

....

....

Choose two of those thoughts and rewrite them in a compassionate manner. For example, if I wrote "fat," I might think about the energy that fat brings to my body, the food that I enjoy eating, and so on.

....

....

....

....

....

....

For this meditation, focus on doing deep belly breaths, with equal inhales and exhales. As you inhale, push your belly out like there is a balloon in your belly. As you exhale, bring your belly button back toward your spine. Repeat this breathing, focusing on the rise and fall of your belly. Each time your mind wanders, bring it back to your breathing. Aim for at least 10 minutes.

Reflect on how you feel following this practice.

What have you learned about your body to this point? Write down as much as you can, reflecting on what you recognize more as you have focused attention on your body.

Sometimes we become aware of our heart pounding when we have intense anxiety, but it is there all the time, constantly beating. How beautiful is that? For today's meditation, just focus on the beating of your heart. As we build a stronger meditation practice, we can actually speed up or slow down our heart. That is the power of the mind–body connection.

What came up for you as you thought about your heart?

An aspect of meditation we have not talked about much yet is exercise. Many practitioners of meditation also practice tai chi, yoga, or some other form of body movement. In fact, we know that exercise is the most effective treatment for depression and anxiety.

What is your physical exercise routine?

....

....

....

....

Are you willing or able to commit to either starting a routine or adding to an existing one? Write the pros and cons of starting or adding, depending on your circumstances.

PROS	CONS

The types of food we consume have an impact on our physical sensations and anxiety. The best example is caffeine. When I consume caffeine, my body gets revved up, and this mimics the physical sensations of anxiety. Other examples include foods high in sugar, alcohol, and mind-altering substances. When we consume, we feel.

Write down all foods that you ate today.
Describe any particular sensations
you felt after eating them.

Mindful eating is a meditative practice that improves your relationship with food and can improve digestion. During one meal today, shut everything off. No phones, no TV, no music, and no talking. Think about where the food came from and how it was prepared. Focus on the smells, tastes, and textures, and just eat.

How was it to practice mindful eating?
What thoughts arose while you ate?

....

....

....

....

....

....

....

....

....

....

....

....

When I am stressed or after I have had an unhealthy anxiety experience, I will often turn to food to comfort me. At other times I do not want to eat at all. Many of us have these behaviors.

Write down the foods you find most comforting. What about them makes you feel this way? Next time you reach for one of these foods, do so without judgment. Anything in moderation is okay.

Whatever your religious belief, try repeating a prayer about food before you eat. Allow me to introduce you to the Meal Gatha that Buddhism teaches to be recited before each meal:

FIRST, SEVENTY-TWO LABORS HAVE BROUGHT US THIS FOOD. WE SHOULD KNOW WHERE IT COMES FROM.

SECOND, AS WE RECEIVE THIS OFFERING WE SHOULD CONSIDER WHETHER OUR VIRTUE AND PRACTICE DESERVE IT.

THIRD, AS WE DESIRE THE MIND TO BE FREE FROM CLINGING, WE MUST BE FREE FROM GREED.

FOURTH, TO SUPPORT OUR LIFE, WE RECEIVE THIS FOOD.

FIFTH, TO REALIZE THE WAY, WE ACCEPT THIS FOOD.

Do you have a practice before eating?
What do you think about the Meal Gatha?

....

....

....

....

Food is essential and keeps us alive, but it can also take control of us. The healthier we eat, the better we feel, and the easier we respond to intense feelings of anxiety.

Earlier this week, I asked you to write down what you ate that day. What have you learned since about your relationship with food?

....

....

....

....

....

....

....

....

....

....

....

....

....

While either seated or standing, take a deep breath and focus on the feelings of your feet on the floor. Slowly shift your focus to one foot and work your way up one side of your body, pausing to notice any sensations you feel in parts of your legs, arms, torso, and head, before working your way down the other side of your body, to the other foot.

How did this body scan feel compared to the one you did a few weeks ago?

All of us can improve aspects of our lives, including what we eat. Think about aspects of your diet you could improve. They could be small changes, like drinking fewer sodas or no sugar before noon. Or you could make a larger nutritional change by reducing your weekly carbohydrate intake. Write down some nutritional changes you could be open to making.

....
....
....
....
....

Does food create anxiety for you? Does the thought of changing your diet create anxiety?

....
....
....
....
....

Today, sit for 15 minutes in proper posture, with your shoulders above your hips and your knees above your ankles. Focus on remaining still, and see if you can notice when you have an urge to shift. The more we become aware of these urges, the more we become able to let them pass and remain still.

What do you notice when you try to fight an urge to move and remain still?

....

....

....

....

....

....

....

....

....

....

....

....

....

We drown out the noise of our mind and body with food, music, TV, exercise, or other distractions. To be still is to be peaceful.

Find peace today in stillness. Try being still for 10 to 15 minutes. What did you notice in stillness?

....

....

....

....

....

....

....

....

....

....

....

....

....

....

I often find that clients or students of meditation are always thinking about what they need to accomplish or how they are "wasting time." Those are judgments. Let them go.

What are some of your judgmental thoughts about the meditation practices or the role that stillness plays in your life?

....

....

....

....

....

....

....

....

....

....

....

....

....

One practice we can use to raise awareness of our senses is to list five noises you can hear, five things you can feel, and five things you can see. The actual practice for tolerating anxiety is to start with five, then four, then three, then two, then one. Play with this during your meditation today. Attempt to meditate for 15 minutes.

Write what you heard, felt, and saw, once you are done.

Part of becoming in touch with your body is learning to love it as it is. That includes when it is healthy, unhealthy, injured, strong, weak, and so on. Often we need to be still and rest. That is when healing can occur.

What thoughts or feelings come up when you are still and not rushing around?

....

....

....

....

....

....

....

....

....

....

....

....

....

....

When was the last time you did nothing? That means not using a phone, computer, or tablet; not talking or reading; not watching TV or listening to music; and not eating. You were doing nothing. This is the practice of just being. Similarly, meditation is also about being.

Today, just be. As you meditate for about 15 minutes, allow thoughts and distractions to drift away. After, reflect on your experience.

....

....

....

....

....

....

....

....

....

....

....

....

....

Meditation can help quiet the mind and improve the health of our body. Stillness is the practice of letting go of to-do's and goals. It requires the relinquishing of control and might feel challenging initially. As with anything new, it requires patience, curiosity, and practice.

Reflect on how patient, curious, and committed you have been to this point.

We must sleep; this is when our body does its best recovering. Research has shown that the less anxious we are, the better we sleep. On the contrary, when we are anxious, we do not sleep well.

WHAT ARE THREE WORDS YOU WOULD USE TO DESCRIBE YOUR SLEEP HABITS?

....

ON AVERAGE, HOW MANY HOURS DO YOU SLEEP PER NIGHT?

....

WHAT TIME DO YOU USUALLY GO TO BED? WHAT TIME DO YOU WAKE UP?

....

....

HOW DO YOU FEEL AFTER A NIGHT OF POOR SLEEP?

....

....

....

....

....

....

....

Have you ever done yoga? Whether you have an advanced practice or have never done it, the following three poses can help you meditate with your body. Choose one pose and hold it for as long as you can. Have no judgment. Just hold the pose, and notice, breathe, and observe.

How did it feel to hold this pose?

You do not have to become the world's best meditator or yogi. Just try to create some time to be selfish and heal your body. It does not matter how good you are at meditation; it just matters that you practice it. Today, let go of *how* you are doing and simply continue *doing*.

How do you feel you have been doing so far?

....

....

....

....

....

....

....

....

....

....

....

....

....

....

When you exercise, you use that period of time to focus and just exercise. You let go of thoughts about your goals for working out, consider listening to music (or not), and just do your routine. Much like when you exercise, when you meditate you can be active *and* focused.

What were some of the thoughts that came up for you while meditating today?

Research has shown that our use of social media is negatively impacting the quality of our sleep and our overall sense of anxiety. Write three intentions you have about improving your sleep and addressing your social media use by the time you finish this book.

SLEEP INTENTION	SOCIAL MEDIA INTENTION
I plan to get to bed earlier this week.	I plan to turn off my phone a half hour before I go to bed.

Some people think the saying "my body, my temple" is just for "gym rats" or people with 5 percent body fat. Nope. Treating our body like a temple is about acknowledging its strengths and weaknesses. None of us is perfect, and none of us has a perfect body, but as you meditate today, think of your body as your temple.

What was today's meditation like, thinking about your body in an accepting manner?

As we near the end of this part of the book, think about the work you have done in reflecting on your body, anxiety, and meditation. Journal about the connection between these ideas and what you have noticed up to this point.

....

....

....

....

....

....

....

....

....

....

....

....

....

....

....

The benefits of meditation include reduced anxiety and depression, increased body awareness, a boosted immune system, increased positivity, early detection of disease, and a quieted mind. These benefits manifest over time, as you will notice as you build the practice of meditation.

*Reflect on any changes to your body
you have noticed up to this point.*

....

....

....

....

....

....

....

....

....

....

....

....

As we have seen from body scans, sometimes there are areas of our body that are injured or need extra care. Picture your body in a perfectly balanced state as you meditate today for 15 to 20 minutes. (If you cannot meditate this long, that is okay. Do the right amount of time for you.)

How balanced did you see your body?

No relationship is perfect—there are always ups and downs. That applies to our relationship with our body as well. At times we feel like Hercules, while at other times we feel weak. By building a relationship with your body, you learn that you are not what you feel.

Describe your current relationship with your body.

"I AM NOT WHAT I FEEL."

Seat yourself comfortably and rest your hands on your lap. Begin to breathe gently. Center yourself in your breath and feel yourself slow down. Ground your awareness back in the present moment, as needed.

How long do you find yourself meditating at this point in the book? Do you find it becoming easier to meditate?

....

....

....

....

....

....

....

....

....

....

....

How do you feel your time commitment and meditation practice are coming along?

....

....

....

....

....

....

With performance psychology, I work with clients on process as opposed to outcome. Reread what you wrote above. Was it mostly focused on outcome (like grading your meditation performance)? Now, try writing about process (e.g., time commitment, posture, defusing thoughts, relationship with anxiety, and so on).

....

....

....

....

....

....

As you meditate today, think about your body. Tune in to your body while taking a few breaths and settling into the current moment. Observe any feelings of tension, warmth, and lightness. Express gratitude to your body for supporting you in your life.

How do you think a healthy body creates a healthy soul?

Focus on your posture as you meditate today, this coming week, and even while sitting in a meeting, eating at the table, or driving. With intention, sit with a strong, open heart and a straight spine.

How is the process of improving your meditation posture going? Sometimes we just need gentle reminders.

The diagram below illustrates the energy points used in Eastern medicine, known as chakras. The study of chakras began in India, around 1500 BCE. They became known in the West due to the popularity of yoga.

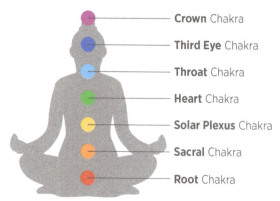

- **Crown** Chakra
- **Third Eye** Chakra
- **Throat** Chakra
- **Heart** Chakra
- **Solar Plexus** Chakra
- **Sacral** Chakra
- **Root** Chakra

One way to think of these points is as areas where energy comes in and goes out. When our body is weak, often it is caused by our body holding on to emotional trauma, not necessarily due to anything medical, nutritional, or otherwise.

Describe where in your body you feel anxiety. Does it align with the location of one or more chakras?

....

....

....

....

....

Today, as you sit, pay attention to the area at the base of your spine (the location of the root chakra) and just observe. Simply sit, align your spine, and observe the feeling of your behind on the seat. Close your eyes. Allow any thoughts or emotions that do not serve you to be released into the ground beneath you with each exhaled breath.

What sensations did you notice as you focused on the root chakra today?

....

....

....

....

....

....

....

....

....

....

....

....

No one can physically see chakras, but that does not mean they do not exist. If you are open to the idea that energy exists (an idea rooted in science), then try to be open to the idea that your energy affects how you feel (e.g., your anxiety).

Have you heard of chakras before this week?
What do you think of chakras now?

....

....

....

....

....

....

....

....

....

....

....

....

....

Using the diagram provided earlier this week, try to sit and pay attention to each of the chakras. Think about each of the seven areas along your spine, and pause for a moment to hold your awareness at each. Repeat the process as you sit for about 20 minutes.

What did you notice as you focused on your spine during today's meditation?

....
....
....
....
....
....
....
....
....
....
....
....
....

Neurology has taught us that our spine is the central highway of nerves in our body. There is no question how important it is and that energy exists in it. Notice if you are able to connect to that energy.

How did you do yesterday focusing on the seven chakras along your spine? (Remember to focus on process and not outcome.)

....
....
....
....
....
....
....
....
....
....
....
....
....

Today, find a meditation practice that allows you to let go of nega-tivity. Weakness is often due to stagnant or negative energy (that is actually the diagnosis in traditional Chinese medicine). Moving energy or releasing it creates new opportunities for us to feel joy and connect with others more deeply. Focus on letting go of negativity for about 25 minutes.

What negativity are you holding on to? The act of writing about it can often help to release it.

We have now completed the mind and body sections of this journal. Continue to notice and practice with both as we move on. In the next section, we will prepare the spirit, which is the foundation of the clinical work I do with clients (especially those working with feelings of anxiety).

Check in with your body now. Have you noticed any changes working through the body prompts over the past few weeks?

PART THREE
SPIRIT

All of us have spirit. Some of us connect with it during our lives, while others continually seek that connection. The spirit can be viewed as your consciousness, soul, energy, or religious beliefs. This section of the book will foster connection with your spirit, digging deeper and going beyond the mind and body.

Our actions impact how we feel, in mind, body, and spirit. An important part of meditation is bringing into intention why we do things, what is important to do, and how to prioritize.

Today, think about what is most important to you. Below are some common values. Rank these values from 1 to 10 in terms of their importance in your life.

____ Family

____ Romance

____ Parenting

____ Friends and social life

____ Work

____ Education and training (knowledge)

____ Recreation and fun

____ Spirituality

____ Community

____ Self-care

How do you feel when you are doing something that you do not want to do?

....

....

....

How do you feel when you are helping someone else?

....

....

....

Today's meditation is about contemplating what *your* values are and what has been bestowed upon you from family, culture, societal pressures, or elsewhere.

Write down the top five words you would use to describe your why (they can be people, places, things, animals, and so on).

1. ....

2. ....

3. ....

4. ....

5. ....

Choose one of those words and meditate on it today. Hold it within your mind's eye and notice any thoughts and feelings that come up for you.

What did you uncover about what your why is?

....

....

....

....

....

Values are like trips with detours. Just because you veer off the planned course, it does not mean that you have gotten lost.

Today, write a letter to yourself regarding a time when you felt you had gotten off course, or lost.

....

....

....

....

....

....

....

....

....

....

....

....

....

....

Earlier this week, you wrote down the top five words that came to mind as you thought about why you do things. Write those words in the left column below. Then, in the right column, list which value (from Day 1, page 106) is linked with each word.

As you meditate today, consider, without judgment, each of these whys and values and the role they play in your life.

YOUR WHY	LINKED VALUES

When we go off course or get lost, there is almost always something we can learn. Earlier this week (page 108), you wrote a letter to yourself about a time when you went off course.

Today, reflect on what you learned from that experience.

What does it mean to follow your values? It might mean taking a flight you are nervous about, changing jobs, or ending a relationship. Consider the idea of following your values as you sit and meditate today.

What did you discover about following your values? What steps can you take to start or continue following them?

See if you can commit to adding a little more time to your meditation practice in the coming week. At least 20 minutes per day is a helpful target (but even 5 minutes is better than none). Find your sweet spot.

Reflect on what your time commitment is at this point.

How have you felt when you acted morally, or with intention? Meditation and a commitment to moral living can have a strong, positive impact on one's health. Write about a time you acted with pure intention. Were there any physical sensations you experienced?

When we are kids, we are taught what is right and what is wrong. As we get older, some of those principles are lost, while some remain intact. Think about where your moral compass is within your life.

As you meditate today (ideally up to 25 minutes), consider where your moral compass has guided you, without judgment. Allow any judging thoughts to pass through your mind without resistance.

What did you discover during this meditation?

If you have noticed that you could be doing better or perhaps you recently acted in a manner that you are not proud of, that is okay. These exercises are not about judging; rather, they are reminders to commit to a better version of yourself.

How would you judge your morals today?

....

....

....

....

....

....

*Write two intentions to act morally
that you can commit to this week.*

....

....

....

....

....

....

Most of us find our way to meditation as a means to manage suffering. As you meditate today, think about what it is that you hope to gain from meditation. Meditation was developed to end suffering for ourselves *and for others*. As you meditate today, think about others in your life who might benefit from the release from suffering.

Who did you think of?

Meditation can be seen as selfish. Time to be alone. Away from loved ones. Unavailable. To release *your* suffering. Working toward enlightenment. These are seemingly selfish acts. However, integrating some work to end others' suffering adds depth to the practice.

How might the people who came up in yesterday's meditation benefit from the release from suffering?

....

....

....

....

....

....

....

....

....

....

....

....

....

As you meditate today, highlight one of the people you were asked to think about the other day, or someone different. Let your mind wander. Each time it does, bring it back to that person and reflect on their suffering. Our connections with others benefit us.

How was this meditation for you today?

This week we reflected on the role of morals in meditation. Indirectly, we were also practicing empathy for others, through the lens of moral action. Thinking about others can enrich our practice.

Where are you in your practice at this point?

According to the Merriam-Webster dictionary, *compassion* is the "sympathetic consciousness of others' distress together with a desire to alleviate it." Research has proven that showing compassion for others can create a positive mental state about how we see ourselves and others.

How do you define compassion? Who are some of the people in your life you show compassion to? Reflect on how you feel when expressing compassion or doing something for these people.

....

....

....

....

....

....

....

....

....

....

....

....

As you meditate today, mentally compose a letter to one of the people you wrote about yesterday. If there was no one, can you think of anyone, or another being, who could benefit from compassion? Focus on words of caring, on their suffering, and how you think their life could be without that suffering.

After your meditation, write
out your letter to them.

Many people will probably come to mind as you go through this week. In meditation, everything is seen as a teacher—even our anxiety. These people, along with our anxiety, may drive us wild from time to time.

We have practiced nonjudgment in this book. Today, think about and reflect on judgments involving these people, your anxiety, or anything that "drives you wild."

Consider opening your heart as you meditate today. As you sit tall, spine straight, think about opening your chest so that your heart is just slightly over your pelvic bone. The practice of compassion allows for us to connect with others more deeply and creates new space for us to cultivate inner peace and self-compassion. Engage with these feelings as you meditate today for about 15 to 20 minutes.

Once you are done, reflect on the practice of opening your heart.

Self-compassion is being compassionate with yourself when you are feeling inadequate, during moments of failure, or during your suffering. How compassionate toward yourself are you?

....

....

....

....

....

....

What have you learned thus far about compassion, and how do you see it affecting you in your life? What steps might you take to improve how you practice self-compassion?

....

....

....

....

....

....

One of the core components of compassion is accepting that we all suffer. Today, as you meditate, think about your own suffering. Think beyond your identity with anxiety. Breathe around those thoughts and feelings by focusing on the inhale and the exhale. Rather than push those thoughts away, allow them to pass on their own.

Once you have completed your meditation, reflect on your attachment to suffering.

Author Kristen Neff has identified three core elements of self-compassion (which is also directly connected to compassion): self-kindness, common humanity, and mindfulness.

Before moving on to next week, reflect on how these three elements fit into your life.

Many of my clients describe feeling out of their bodies, as though they are watching themselves through an anxious lens. What if we saw that experience as spiritual rather than flawed? Though many of us believe that anxiety is dangerous, no one has ever died from anxiety. The ability to feel your body, even in anxious times, brings life.

How might you see your anxiety
as part of your spirit?

....
....
....
....
....
....
....
....
....
....
....
....
....

If you're religious, have you ever rushed through prayers to get to the end? Today, commit to your meditation practice. No matter your religious or spiritual identity, truly commit to it rather than just going through the motions. Aim for 20 minutes.

What did you notice when you commit to the practice rather than just doing it as a habit?

....

....

....

....

....

....

....

....

....

....

....

....

....

What do you think is the difference
between religion and spirituality?

....

....

....

....

....

....

Academically speaking, they are quite similar. The main difference
is that religion is organized, with deities, and spirituality allows for
flexibility and individuality. They can also be polarizing—if I am
religious, I may judge those who identify as spiritual, and vice versa.

Today, reflect on practicing
accepting things as they are.

....

....

....

....

....

....

If we are religious, we have likely been taught about a holy being and how to worship it. In meditation, we can be flexible about whether the *g* in *god* is capitalized, what essential nature is, and so on. As you meditate today, think about the word *deity*. You could repeat it or call to your mind the image of your deity. Be creative with the thoughts and feelings that come up for you.

For how long did you meditate on the word deity? How did that go?

In meditation, we often think of "who" is sitting here. This is where the practice becomes more philosophical. In relation to your religious or spiritual practice, who are you? Write down your nonjudgmental response.

....

....

....

....

....

No matter our beliefs, unless we have committed murder or other egregious acts, we are often accepted as sinners or people who suffer. It is through prayer (or meditation) that we can assist in ending that.

How are you about judging yourself against others?

....

....

....

....

....

As you meditate today (aiming for at least 20 minutes, if possible), connect with your heart area as you have done previously. This time, however, think about your spirit behind your heart. Does it have a specific shape? Is it cool or warming to the touch?

Once you are done, reflect on this experience and write about how you would describe your spirit.

....
....
....
....
....
....
....
....
....
....
....
....
....

As we foster a relationship with our deeper self—our spirit—we keep diving deeper. This can be scary at times, but the goal is to keep diving. How deep have you been diving into your self as you have worked through this book?

People's motivations shift, and motivation is part of feeding the spirit. Often people become motivated by the start of a new year. But we do not have to wait until then.

Write out some new year's resolutions you have made in the past. Describe how they progressed (without judgment). Notice any anxiety that arises over these resolutions.

We are motivated by things that make us feel good on the inside (intrinsic motivation) and by tangible byproducts (extrinsic motivation). While getting money, gifts, loyalty points, and trophies feels good, evaluating intrinsic motivation gets you closer to the core of your spirit. Intrinsic motivation connects with our sense of self, personal growth, and recognition of our purpose. Think about these three things as you meditate today (for at least 20 minutes).

What came up for you while meditating?

If you are like most people I work with, you might feel some guilt or shame about the extrinsic motivators listed yesterday (money, gifts, and so on). Releasing judgment is part of meditation. We are not connected to material items, and we can release judgment of our desire to obtain them.

Consider evaluating your motivations today. What are your judgments about being motivated by extrinsic factors?

In the table below, list your top intrinsic and extrinsic motivations.

INTRINSIC	EXTRINSIC

Choose any of these motivations and notice, as you meditate today, how your mind and body feel when you think about them. After, write down your observations.

....

....

....

....

....

*What have you learned about
your motivation this week?*

....

....

....

....

....

*Now, think and write about what you might
be willing to change. See if you can shift from
the extrinsic motivations and place more
emphasis on the intrinsic motivations. As we
have seen, this helps us get closer to the spirit.*

....

....

....

....

....

....

Many of us do not do well with change. For example, as you have gone through this book, you may have noticed how challenging it is to let go of anxiety. I preach that "Change is good." Today, as you meditate, use this mantra: *Change is good*.

What do you think about the idea of change?

....

....

....

....

....

....

....

....

....

....

....

....

....

When we run from a situation that causes us anxiety, that retreat gives more power to the anxiety, making it stronger. Our goal is to stare our fears in the eye, and they may include things that we are not terribly proud of. Learning to accept things as they are creates space for change, which can help alleviate anxiety and create inner peace.

Which motivations from this week do you feel require the most attention?

*We are able to experience joy in our spirit,
even when things feel dismal. What do you
feel in your body when you experience joy?
What thoughts do you have when you feel joy?
How do you think joy impacts your spirit?*

....

....

....

....

....

....

*Describe a time in the past 5 to 10 years
when you physically felt joy.*

....

....

....

....

....

....

....

When I first learned meditation, one of my teachers instructed me to hold a small smile while sitting. It felt strange. Then, as I got deeper into the practice, I noticed that a smile could change how I felt. As you meditate today, breathing naturally and with your eyes closed, think of something that brings you joy—and smile.

How did that feel? Did you notice a change in your body by adding the smile?

....
....
....
....
....
....
....
....
....
....
....
....

Creating joy in life can be an effort, but the benefits are endless. When we feel anxiety, it can be difficult to smile, but anxious moments are when a smile—or even better, a good laugh—can do the most good.

When was the last time you had a really good laugh? What prompted it?

....

....

....

....

....

....

....

....

....

....

....

....

Maya Angelou wrote, "A joyful spirit is evidence of a grateful heart." Because of our anxiety, sometimes we forget about gratitude. As you meditate today, think about what you are grateful for. Think about why you feel this appreciation. With every inhale and exhale of your breath, mentally say *thank you*.

Reflect on what you were grateful for. How did it feel to meditate on that today?

Sometimes people suffering from anxiety also experience moments of sadness. At these times, it becomes more difficult to feel joy. Create a pie chart below to illustrate how much time you spend feeling joy compared to sadness.

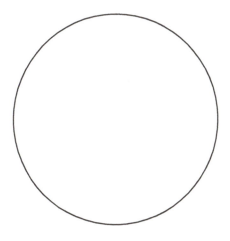

Describe two small steps you are willing to take today to create more joy in your life.

....

....

....

....

....

....

As you meditate today, imagine the sensation of joy as a spark of light within the body. As you breathe, visualize that light expanding in size and allow this sensation to spread throughout your body. Imagine any lingering negative feelings melting away in the light of this joy.

What did you notice as you tried to connect with the sensation of joy?

Meditation is the beginning of connecting with your joyful spirit. Sometimes I forget how simple things are, and then I spend time with a puppy or a young child. Their focus is tiny. Their needs are minimal. And their joy is palpable.

Describe some possible activities that might help transform your joy. Consider committing to one of these activities this week.

Some philosophies study auras of color around people. I once asked a colleague, "What do you think about when you hear the word *spirit*?" They answered, "Yellow. Brightness, like bright yellow and other colors." They later described a feeling of happiness thinking about their spirit and this color.

What is your favorite color? Is that the same color you would use to describe your spirit? How do you think that color connects with your spirit?

....

....

....

....

....

....

....

....

....

....

....

....

As you meditate today, imagine a rainbow. See if the color you wrote about yesterday stands out. As you inhale, try to visualize each color of the rainbow one at a time, then together in harmony. What do you feel in response to each color? As you exhale, let go of any negative emotions that do not serve you in a positive way.

Once you are done, reflect on this experience below.

Altruism is often described as doing something for the greater good, without expecting something in return. Consider the welfare of others and imagine the colors you might see. For example, if you were walking through an impoverished area with homelessness, you might not see bright yellow, reflecting joy and light. Instead, you might see shades of gray, or even black, reflecting the suffering in the community.

What do you think of this notion?

As you sit in your meditation today, think about unselfish regard for others. When we close our eyes, we can see light or images; a lot is happening. Try to practice with the brightness and see if you can make it brighter with each inhaled breath.

Were you able to see changes in the brightness as you meditated? What does unselfish regard in meditation mean to you?

....

....

....

....

....

....

....

....

....

....

....

....

Consider the process of exploring the role of mind, body, and spirit in relation to your anxiety. As we near the end of this journey together, reflect on your progress to this point.

You were courageous when you took the first step of opening this book, then doing the practices. This might not have been your first attempt to deal with your anxiety, and it likely will not be your last. That is human nature. We explore. We try. We fail. We succeed. We keep going. Meditate with a message of gratitude for your ongoing efforts.

Having arrived at this point in the book, what are you grateful for?

Before we begin our last week of prompts, take a moment to pause and reflect. The abstract design below is for you to color, scribble in, or just stare at. An important part of meditation as we build a healthier relationship with our anxiety is to pause and reflect.

As we conclude these weeks together, let us reflect on our mind, our body, and our spirit.

Without judgment, describe what have you noticed about each by working through this book.

MIND

....

....

BODY

....

....

SPIRIT

....

....

As you go through life, especially in moments of unhealthy anxiety, consider which of these three aspects is at play. Are your thoughts creating the anxiety (mind), are you attaching to physical sensations (body), or are you burned out and drained (spirit)?

....

....

Today is a time to recharge. Think about your mind, body, and spirit as you meditate. As you breathe, notice if any of them feel off balance. Release any tension you may be holding with each exhale, and invite a feeling of relaxation to spread across your being, starting from the top of your head and moving down through your body to your feet.

How did you feel about recharging yourself today? For how long are you meditating now?

At the beginning of this book, we discussed three main behaviors when engaging in a meditation practice: patience, curiosity, and commitment. Define each term as it relates to your life.

PATIENCE

....
....
....
....

CURIOSITY

....
....
....
....

COMMITMENT

....
....
....
....

Our mind is wired in such a way that we can do only one thing at a time. So for all you multitaskers out there, let it go!

For today's meditation, choose to think about patience, curiosity, or commitment. In your mind's eye, reflect on its meaning in your life (as you wrote about yesterday), without judgment.

When you are done (after 25 to 30 minutes, if possible), write down what came up for you.

The changes brought about by meditation are not immediate. However, be assured that engaging in meditation *will* promote significant changes, so focus on the process. When we focus on the outcome, we are judging.

For today, simply focus on the process of working through this book. How has the process of working through this book been for you?

....

....

....

....

....

....

....

....

....

....

....

....

It is not becoming the best meditator that creates positive change. Just five minutes a day could change your life. On this, our second-to-last day in this journal, think about choosing to be committed to your meditation practice. Meditate for as long as you comfortably can.

What are some barriers interfering with your commitment to your meditation practice? Write them below. Once you raise your awareness of these barriers, you can potentially head them off.

Patience. Curiosity. Commitment. These three components of practicing connection to the mind, body, and spirit cultivate peace in your life. We all want peace. On this last day, reflect on each of these components, and describe how you have demonstrated each quality throughout your practice in this book:

PATIENCE

....

....

....

....

CURIOSITY

....

....

....

....

COMMITMENT

....

....

....

....

Parting Words

Some of you may have found this book to be difficult, others easy, and some unhelpful. All of these reactions are okay. I often tell clients that if meditation was easy, and if the benefits were immediate, we would all do it. There would also be greater peace. However, meditation is difficult, and this 21st century involves technology, distractions, and avoidance. We reward busyness and constant connection. We are focused on technology and medicine, but meditation has been used as a form of medicine for the ages. The variables of this life create anxiety; in fact, they likely have created a society that normalizes what it means to be an "anxious person." This book and your courage to practice meditation are my motivations for my professional work. I am thankful to work with humans through their suffering and provide guidance for tools to reduce the pain. We all suffer, but why suffer all the time?

Remember to remain patient or notice when you are acting impatient. Practice openness and curiosity to experiences and commit to this practice. It is natural that the relationship will ebb and flow, just like anxiety does. We do not feel intense anxiety all day, all the time, every day. It comes and goes. That too might be how you find your relationship with meditation. As long as you recall that this life is about connecting your mind, body, and spirit while remaining patient, curious, and committed, I am confident that you will feel peace.

~urces

The Counseling and Wellness Center, LLC
(TheCWNJ.com/counseling)
A guide to the more popular theoretical orientations for mental health

Mindfulness-based stress reduction (MBSR)
(MBSTraining.com/jon-kabat-zinn/)
Further information on Jon Kabat-Zinn and his work on MBSR

Healthline: "Effects of Anxiety on the Body."
(Healthline.com/health/anxiety/effects-on-body)
An overview of the major effects anxiety has on the body

University of Minnesota: Taking Charge of Your Health and Wellbeing:
"What Do Specific Foods Do?"
(TakingCharge.csh.umn.edu/explore-healing-practices/food-medicine/
what-do-specific-foods-do)
A resource to learn more about how foods can affect anxiety

Healthline: "A Beginner's Guide to the 7 Chakras and Their Meanings."
(Healthline.com/health/fitness-exercise/7-chakras)
A concise explanation of each of the seven main chakras

Calm (Calm.com)
One of many applications that provide meditation cues

References

Alvaro, P.K., R.M. Roberts, and J.K. Harris. "A Systematic Review
Assessing Bidirectionality between Sleep Disturbances, Anxiety,
and Depression." *Sleep* 35, no. 7 (2013): 1059–1068.
DOI:org/10.5665/sleep.2810.

Delmonte, M.M. "Meditation and Anxiety Reduction: A Literature
Review." *Clinical Psychology Review* 5, no. 2 (1985): 91–102.

Hoge, E.A., E. Bui, S.A. Palitz, N.R. Schwarz, M.E. Owens, J.M. Johnston,
and N.M. Simon. "The Effect of Mindfulness Meditation Training on
Biological Acute Stress Responses in Generalized Anxiety Disorder."
Psychiatry Research 262 (2018): 328–332.

Kabat-Zinn, J. *Full Catastrophe Living: Using the Wisdom of
Your Body and Mind to Face Stress, Pain, and Illness.* New York,
NY: Delacort, 1990.

Ludwig, D.S., and J. Kabat-Zinn. "Mindfulness in Medicine." *JAMA* 300,
no. 11 (2008): 1350–1352. DOI:10.1001/jama.300.11.1350.

Merriam-Webster. "Compassion." Accessed December 20, 2020.
Merriam-Webster.com/dictionary/compassion.

Neff, K.D. (2003). "The Development and Validation of a Scale to
Measure Self-compassion." *Self and Identity* 2 no. 3 (2003):
223–250. DOI:10.1080/15298860309027.

Rodriguez-Carvajal, R., C. Garcia-Rubio, D. Paniagua, G. Garcia-Diex,
and S. de Rivas. "Mindfulness Integrative Model (MIM): Cultivating
Positive States of Mind Towards Oneself and the Others through
Mindfulness and Self-Compassion." *Anales De Psicologia/Annals of
Psychology* 32, no. 3 (2016): 749–760.

L., B.M. Hoffman, P.J. Smith, and J.A. Blumenthal. "Exercise atment for Anxiety: Systematic Review and Analysis." *Annals Behavioral Medicine: A Publication of the Society of Behavioral Medicine* 49, no. 4 (2015): 542–556. DOI:10.1007/s12160-014-9685-9.

Woods, H.C., and H. Scott. "Sleepyteens: Social Media Use in Adolescence is Associated with Poor Sleep Quality, Anxiety, Depression and Low Self-esteem." *Journal of Adolescence* 51 (2016): 41–49. DOI:/10.1016/j.adolescence.2016.05.008.

Acknowledgments

I have gratitude for my own journey with anxiety and of course, Robert Kennedy Roshi, who continues to influence my meditation practice. I am hopeful we continue to find peace, together.

About the Author

Peter J. Economou, PhD, ABPP, is a licensed psychologist, an associate professor at the Graduate School of Applied and Professional Psychology at Rutgers University for the graduate programs in applied psychology, certified by the American Board of Professional Psychology in cognitive behavioral therapy (CBT), and certified by the Association of Applied Sport Psychology. Dr. Pete is the founder of the Counseling & Wellness Center, LLC, which is a clinical practice specializing in CBT. He is an active member of state and national associations, and is a contributor to media outlets. Dr. Pete's research focuses on third wave CBT, including mindfulness and meditation, multicultural psychology, and performance psychology. As a student of Zen Buddhism, Dr. Pete has been studying at the Morning Star Zendo with Robert Kennedy Roshi for several years and integrates Eastern spiritual practices into Western behavioral science.

Follow Dr. Pete on Instagram @OfficialDrPete and on Twitter @TheCWCNJ and @OfficialDrPete, and listen to his podcast, *When East Meets West*.

CPSIA information can be obtained
at www.ICGtesting.com
Printed in the USA
JSHW021024090621
15650JS00003B/3